For M

ISBN: 978-1-915760-50-0

Cover designed by Aaron Kent

Edited by: Aaron Kent & Cathleen Allyn Conway

Typeset by Aaron Kent

Broken Sleep Books Ltd   Broken Sleep Books Ltd
Rhydwen   Fair View
Talgarreg   St Georges Road
Ceredigion   Cornwall
SA44 4HB   PL26 7YH

Contents

2024

The men have decided
they've given up too much,
it started with podcasts:

> *Women can't eat bread and expect us to fuck them, right bro?*
> *They just want us to suck their farts*
> *and drink their bath water, right bro?*

She lifts up a rock
in the Manosphere
and finds a million squirming micro gurus
one man decides that time is stupid   *right bro*
he wants to punch the sun!
Invents his own clock,
instead of 24 hours being one day
his days are 6-hour blocks (Why?)
In just ONE of your days I've already had FOUR! crushing it   right bro

He holds up his meatypink fingers to emphasise four.
Another man eats nothing but heifer
squeezes milk from a teat
directly into the mouth of his son.
Another man drinks his own peepee.

Is it the spectre of post-viral fatigue?
She keeps this thought to herself
scared she'll be labelled a tinfoil-hat wearer too.
She finally shaves off her eyebrows
for the private photoshoot
a saucy calendar for her 40th birthday
unwraps the talking dildo,
another gift to herself.

2004

A discovery has been made
about her brain
its reading age
why it lacks speed
the university gives her a therapeutic desktop,
a programme that reads
all her assignments out loud,
she enters bedtime stories for it to speak:
The Tale of the Dirty Princess, The Haunted Teacup.
When she's horny
she chooses a woman's voice
when she wants reassurance, a man's.
Sometimes she inputs nonsense sounds
kklkl prolfka
invents her own language
like when she used to sing Eurovision
in the bath as a child, made noises
into mum's wide-tooth comb
placed bubbles on her chest
white pillowy boobies
imagined away her frizz,
instead, a mane flowing
golden down her back.

1990

A naked body is a face,
the nipples are eyes
belly button a nose
and genitals, the mouth.
She thinks this is the reason
why boys are naturally naughty –
when they are naked
their tongues stick out.
Girls are always polite,
lips clamped shut
downward eyes.

On weekends she trades sweets
for rides on the neighbours' bikes,
a lollipop is worth
10 goes 'round the green flats
a single cola bottle is worth two,
boys are better customers
their mums don't limit their intake.

2002

Two teachers at school
are after the other girls in her art class,
she walks a line between disgust and longing,
makes collages: bombs, nipples
drips liquid latex onto the magazine cut-outs
shiny, wrinkled,
she swipes one of mum's sleeping pills
to stick in the centre of the page.
The model at life drawing
has the biggest cock she will ever lay
her eyes on, swollen slug,
her friends exchange red glances
gripping their nervous charcoal
and his penis stiffens ever so slightly,
they drop the bus fare home in the tip jar.
Out loud she says
if I want to be a r e a l artist
what's the fucking point of A levels?
But at night she studies hard,
a beaver pinching her nose to down coffee
if she doesn't hold all the information
in her head at once
it evaporates like pasta steam.
Her life drawings are back from teacher
marked down for incorrect proportions.

2014

Is it the lack of sleep
the extra hours at work,
a new taste for ale
that bloats her?
Is something in the soil
making her smelly?
Men hold her
a microsecond less in their gaze
direct their conversation
just past her face.
I LOvE a woMAn who fEEls liKe She doEsnt HAve to wer MAKEup
She wants to explain
her issues with fibres,
the dietician
talks over her symptoms.
Says she's overweight
but also that she has lost weight too fast…(?)
then time is up and she leaves
the appointment with nothing
but leaflets and a stern
recommendation for yoghurt.
The first baby friend arrives,
they throw him a mini day rave,
dancing in a loose circle
they pass him round
to get a good sniff
of his yeasty head.

2009

She has never known
so many vacant buildings,
dabs a new powder
to deal with the MDMA drought.
On Sunday mornings she skulks
along the dual carriageway,
another rave in a carpet factory,
sleeps wholesome in her tangerine room
internship abandoned so she can practise being an artist.
She learns to use a Macchinetta,
on weekdays she taps her jobseekers bus pass
visiting every exhibition,
sketchbook empty of drawings
but crammed with instructions
written in white-hot hyperfocus:

bag of poo (installation)

Bingo + Couscous?

Biscuits and juice!!!! (not a shopping list).

"mayonnaise is the king".

Sisyphus but in high heels!!!!!!

Ideas that crumble on second glance
but make her feel as though she is
d o i n g   s o m e t h i n g
b e i n g   s o m e o n e

2001

Shaves a line in her eyebrow
sleeps huddled with her friends
packed tight as a fresh box of B&H
looks for men she can shock
you're only 17 wow
they always pay for her cabs.

1986

Strangers call her a clever boy
fooled by green dungarees, her bald dome
are you a little big man then?
They fling him up in the air, high as he can go.
Eventually a ringlet sprouts
centre stage on her eggshell head
mum clamps it with a plastic bow
what a prettylittlething   what a sweetie.
Chomping on dirt dad slaps an earthworm
from her portly fist
the puddles are suddenly too toxic.

2019

She goes to an evening mushroom retreat
in a repurposed warehouse
led by three girls
who call themselves shamans,
matza-thin yoga mats on the concrete floor
communal salad
hold hands   breathe fast   hard-hard-inin-ouout
The shamans speak like personal trainers
that'sitkeepgoing   breath more aggressive now   hard-hard-inin-ouout
the geezer next to her turns scarlet
snot on her philtrum thick as cow cream
a lady with bunches gags melodically
her head bent over crossed legs
girl in white flares waves a sage stick around
but stubs it out quick – *babes the smoke alarm!*
bangs an upturned bowl instead.
On the way home
she eats two peeled eggs
out of a plastic box
so cold they may as well be choc ices.

1988

She can count up to 10 objects,
she can write her name,
can she stand on one foot
for longer than nine seconds?

At this stage
her brain is like a hard drive
dumping out bits to make room
for the soft and urgent milestones –
putting on her own vest,
drawing a person with a body.

The fading parts of her,
the part that says
apatooty instead of 'absolutely',
the part that cannot hold scissors,
that needs help to poopoo,
are now gone,
belong only to her parents.

There are bigger events happening –
a plane explodes in the sky
a bishop is arrested for kneeling
the neighbours keep a secret woman
locked up in their box room.
No one looks past
the wife's business glasses
the husband's jazzy tie
until one clammy night
the secret woman escapes
runs onto the green in front of the houses
dressed in a moth-eaten t-shirt

screaming wet sounds
smelling of cleaning product.

What is a memory anyway
but a picture that mummy and daddy
tell you to draw
so you can look back on it
one day in your own house
when you finally sort out the boxes
in the loft and see a crumpled paper
with a gingerbread figure
and the word *ME*
written in crayon in its middle?

1993

The others tell Teacher
they heard the bomb blast in bed
middle-of-the-night glass smash,
make exploding gestures
with their hands
following imaginary shrapnel
with their eyebrows.
They are lying, she thinks
she heard nothing,
spent the night staring
at the cottage cheese ceiling
through the mesh of the princess canopy.

That evening she crosses herself
even says *Amen*
(she saw it on *Saved by the Bell*)
knees itchy from the carpet
she tries to speak to God
in her own head
asks if he can please
let her hear the bomb next time.

2012

The world didn't end as predicted.
Flash mobs are spreading
at every station in the city
groups of grown-ups
box step, shoulder roll, clap-clap-jump!
For the finale, an attempt at a grapevine.
Is it team building?
Are they selling a new power juice?
She works at quaint festivals
making decorative tea towels with children,
only eats happy animals,
it's the wettest August on record.
She assumed she'd be in Belize
by now, or Mexico, but she's crawling
on her friend's kitchen floor
left tit hanging out her jumpsuit
acid breath singalong
with her greatest loves
women who speakerbox each other's victories,
sink quiet jealousies,
whose bodies will grow
and shrink cells of life and destruction,
spitting sav blanc
back in the mug she screams
turn up the bass bitch!

2022

In January a ham in the shape of a goldfish goes on sale at the supermarket

In February a nice young family stands in a warehouse surrounded by all their possessions: 80 packets of out-of-date medicine, 207 loose nappies, a bag of teeth

In March she quietly moves away from Boyfriend

In April the neighbour's cat sicks on her shoe: a miniature fatberg of papers, breath mints, a still-alive mouse

In May she re-enters society by presenting a live art performance in a group show, sits on a low stool mixing ketchup with Polyfilla, stuffs the mixture into a piping bag and writes the words I LOVE A WOMAN WHO FEELS LIKE SHE DOESN'T HAVE TO WEAR MAKE UP directly onto the linoleum floor

In June the blackberries are so fat and delicious she gives herself diarrhoea

In July she keeps the windows locked to block the burning rubber of the London wildfires, she contemplates becoming an ice lolly influencer

In August a nation opts into fluffy amnesia (again)

In September young men on Tinder dress themselves like serial killers from the 1980s

In October a woman yells *beef seasoning* into the camera, pours it into the back of a pick-up truck flooded with instant noodles

In November a commoner throws an egg at the king

In December eggs are on ration because all the birds are sick

25

2000

The snake grows larger
with each bite of the apple
the 2 6 8 4 buttons
guide its movement,
she makes a hotbox of her mind
watching people sleep on the telly
You are live on Channel 4, please do not swear.
A great-granny serves her a blend
of cider, larger and blackcurrant,
lads waiting for day labour
on the roadside chuckle at her drunk gait
offer a hand up the curb.
In lessons she heats
a yellow lighter under her desk
to brand a smiley face onto her wrist,
a boy from the blue table
steals another boy's shoes
chucks one in the pond
gives the other back with a wink.

2026

Her network stop employing her
can you still relate to children? not quite suited for the back office
f u c k she calculates
the side-hustle value of her bedroom
strips the cupboard of vintage tracksuits,
mum's porcelain doll, the Nikon from dad,
when did she decide she would be a woman
with a floral tea set? A gang of mismatched coupe glasses?
She has never had a living room big enough to toast 13 people.
She wraps each decorative chopstick
clip-on earring and cottage-core cardigan
in a bloated sigh, as if this bric-a-brac
were real parts of her self that had chipped off
the wood plane and become animated
as she was taking shape.
She contemplates auctioning
the talking dildo to a subsection of followers
who take an itchy interest in her belly button prints.
She siphons the rest from mum and dad
banks on them not needing proper care
and hands it all over to a young woman
who doesn't know that the boat
is worth at least eight grand more
than the asking price.

2027

Even the instigators
regret the smallening
the re-inking of borders
she misses her passport
but not tomatoes.
Every week more gatherings of   *tRUth sEEkers*
mushroom in city parks
each with their own special hobbies.
Some think the moon is a lie
It's one giant candle!
Some think pea protein is made from Christian children.
A young woman is arrested for poisoning the squirrels
THEY'RE NOT REAL she shouts *THEY ARE GOVERNMENT SPIES*
In Arkansas they are building a monument
to all the unborn foetuses
a hoard of *wHoleSomE mOms* in Sunday blazers
gripping tiki lamps.

2028

For winter she moors by a square   that used to be a bank   that used to be a factory   that used to be a floodplain   She snoozes by the window of her boat   writes backwards on the window: *You are live on Channel 4, please do not swear*   Passers-by stop mid stroll on the towpath   watch the slow rise and fall of her chest   she collects handsome tips via a brand new card reader   In an old welly boot she has hidden a camera to steal portraits

young woman with mouth opening
microsecond before
she reaches the peak of a yawn

teen girl slicks edges
in her reflection
doesn't see me at all

husbands with frowning baby
head on woolly shoulder
dried white sick on bib

mum with two
angry daughters

dog eating a Dorito

man with hand in pants

29

1984

On the night of her birth mum watches a TV film:
Young man in blue dungarees plays with pet canaries.
Pregnant woman frantically strips wallpaper.
Family prop mattresses against the window.
F16 fighter jets roar over Yorkshire.
Homemade banner at a CND march:
There can be no defence against nuclear attack
two boys watch from a treetop.
Man with thick lenses sifts through a binder labelled 'War Book'.
Granny in a paisley headscarf heaves boxes of Spam out the corner shop.
French manicured fingers draw a blast radius on a paper map.
Woolworths explodes.
The milk bottles on the doorstep melt.
A silent white frame
then everybody vomits.

2051

Algae blooms have robbed her
the sensation of submergence
in wild water, a whole season
and she can't leave the house
stuck with the whirring neighbour
splayed on the day bed
the drooped song of a starling.
Watching a waterfall reel
on her headset she attempts
a breast stroke on the bathroom tiles
delights in the brief cold against her clavicle.

2005

The man in the baseball cap burns her a CD
he is the owner of the only penis in this town
that hasn't been to the university.
He reminds her of a chicken kiev.
She is poor but not 'poor'
the administrators have provided
just enough free money
she doesn't really need a coat.
She won't trust the free councillor
his shoes are scuffles, he says *issyews*
instead of issues, on the way out
she swipes a box of *tishyous*.

2064

She never learnt to cartwheel.
All the other girls could
but she decided she was too tall,
had too far to reach down
would only trust her hands with other people's load.
What is it like to be a small woman?
To be flipped and tossed like a baton?
Since the age of eight she has been sturdy as a prized cow
understood her place to be the bottom of the pyramid
grew to respect her girth
but she thinks about starting a fire, just once,
so she knows the feeling of being held
like a waif, like a grown-up baby
perhaps the fireman will have a moustache.

2023

A series of non-decisions
leaves her childless
(child*free*?) she needs
to moisturise her hands
more frequently
keeps a miniature
tub of cream in her bag.
Does this mean
she has finally
become a woman?

Beavers have made a comeback!
A couple named
Sean and Ellie
have been released
in Ealing, are put to work
fixing the dams.
She reads an article
about a mouse
with two dads.

The trend for
Tiny Homes is growing,
Start-up companies
will build you a house
for £30,000 to £100,000
depending on finish :)
A man lives in a skip
and Instagrams it,
he has a Ring doorbell.

If you live
on a roadside camp
you face time in prison,
a £2,500 fine
or your home being taken.
The law of trespass
excludes us from 92%
of the land in England.
Every single one
of England's rivers
fail safety standards.
If you come to the UK illegally:
➡ You can't claim asylum
➡ You can't benefit from our modern slavery protections
➡ You can't make spurious human rights claims
➡ You can't stay

2029

Her clitoris is having
a revival, a chirming
queue outside her boat
her sex thrives on disaster
and the trees are on fire.
She gets to know each bee by name,
hosts get togethers for the remaining
water voles, wonders
do squirrels have memories?
She meets a young woman
who forgot to shut the weed hatch,
came home to an empty plot of water
boat sunk but the cat survived
all her beginnings floated away.
Now whenever she rises in the lock
the sick comes with it,
keep boat forward of the cill marker
fingers angry with constant sweat.
Friends a few years ahead warn her
that the fire iron in her gut
will only get hotter.

2021

She used to listen to drum n bass all night,
now she writes *fab!* at the end of emails.
Some of her baby friends can now
hold a sippy cup, remember her by the moon books
she sent in the post. She spends hours
researching if guinea pigs make good pets,
sells prints of her belly button on Esty,
a man with horns occupies the White House.

1999

Mum is convinced she'll go iffy
from the new inoculation
keeps her off school for the day.
For lunch it's just a can
of Diet Pepsi, *thanks.*
In her favourite magazine
a series of yes/no questions direct her
through a bubblegum flowchart
to figure out which 26-year-old man
is her real soulmate:
I usually go for sensitive guys
who write poetry or play the guitar,
*party guys aren't my thing (**yes**/no)*
I like my cutie to dress conservative & preppy,
*I don't care for facial hair, tattoos or body piercings (yes/**no**)*
I like playing games like paintball
or a round of mini golf (what is paintball?)
Too tall to shower standing up
she lies back in the bathtub
gathering a pool under her back
to soak her hair
locks the rubber shower hose
in the web between her toes
so the scalding water spurts out.

2036

Deepfake backlash is reaching climax
for a special treat she develops
a cache of forgotten disposables
stashed in a Kwik Save bag
in mum's and dad's shed

Nan's bruised face
(from the abandoned insurance claim against the bus driver who sped off too soon)

baby on a balcony
plump and pink against the jagged skyline
bank towers gleaming in the distance

group of white teens throwing gang signs

friends in denim dungarees
hanging on a train
flash bounces silver off the bars
the taught skin of armpits

eight bodies in a rain-clogged tent

high-heeled trainers
on a pebble beach

birthday cake shaped into a gingerbread man
number 9 candle sticks out his belly

2030

Her latest series goes viral -
clay models of squirrels in shabby suits
each holding a globe dripping with blood,
the artwork is called *NUt sEEkers.*

She takes her parents on a cruise
a belated everything present,
mojitos mojitos
all you can eat pea protein.
Mum hasn't been on a ship
since she entered the country in '72
when England was boil-in-a-bag
everything, cockroaches,
when dad had a 26-inch waist.

2031

Coots nest on the roof of her boat
a jumble of twigs,
cardboard, a crisp packet,
the white shields extending from their beaks
remind her of the shape of Mr Burns's head.
It's illegal for her to cruise
until the chicks have moved out
she sips beer made from old bread.

Her bank account is thickening
another buyer interested
in her secret photographs of
People on the Towpath,
she has a significant following
but becoming a   s o m e o n e
is more boring than she realised
she toys with the idea of adding
an umlaut to all her vowels
to feel a rush of sophistication.

At weekends she takes
mum and dad out on a dingy,
dad plops a hand in the water
she keeps a close watch so he doesn't bring
the brown muck to his lips.
Remember the BubbleWorks ride
at Chessington World of Adventures?
A trip through Professor Burp's Fizz Factory!
His animatronic eyes, his German accent,
a cow filled with gas floating above a cactus
human bananas drinking cocktails in a jacuzzi,
she screamed at the strobe light climax
and dad covered her eyes with his hand.

2032

She fights with mum
about the most appropriate postcode
to scatter his ashes,
the trees are on fire again
the world is still ending.
To amuse herself she makes clogs
in the shape of giant ostrich feet
fashions them out of driftwood.
Trampling along the river edge at night
she leaves enormous footprints in the silt
the swimmers believe there is some mystery creature
inhabiting the forever-chemical'd river.

2059

Dulled by her need
to keep pushing herself
through the sausage maker,
to water herself daily,
invent new ways
to occupy herself in the cold evenings
she sends slices of bread
that have lived in her slippers
to a fan. In return he sends
tickets to hologram Sugababes.
On the walkway to Wembley
she clocks that the lampposts look like the lollipops
they used to dispense in Ikea.

2037

She makes creatures
with the foster kids
glue-gunning doll heads
to old tins of chocolate milk
for arms they use pencils,
egg box monsters, exquisite misfits.

At the safeguarding assessment
she hid her special art books
from the social worker
scared she'd be marked down
for the glossy pages

self-portrait: 80-year-old nude woman
breast scraping her knee
eyebrow arched as if to say
what you looking at

photo series: two beautiful-sad
women in the back of a taxi
metallic crop tops reflect
dirty evening sun

She lets the children draw
all over them, rip out pages
for messy collages.
In the mornings they sip pear juice
red hair tangled by a miniature tornado
swirling arms on the balcony
copying the wind farms
that guard the hazy estuary
like brave soldiers.

2007

Always the first to need a shit
at night she fizzes like a snow globe
by day she's a balled-out melon,
all of her pals have ruined their bladders.
She joins a pirate radio station
works the freeparty bars
raising money for the aerial
turn up your dials they call it dubstep.
Graduation photos are far too expensive,
a photoshoot with mum
behind the *Keep Off The Grass* sign,
she mock-kisses the decorative roll of paper
buys a gold rimmed frame for Nan's mantle.
Every time a charity fundraiser
stops her in the street she reads
from a specially prepared script:
I already do three sorry,
Médecins sans Frontières,
Plan International and a small one
that looks after Tigers.
She sometimes replaces the tiger charity
with one that buys donkeys
for people who really, really need them.

2033

Her inner   *me*
is like a wild goat on the run
before a tsunami.
She is pushing rubbish
down a chute, she is crossing
the North Circular aqueduct,
she is pressed against the wall
of the tube platform
the edge too alive to get too close to
i have hands, she realises, *and a face!*
i have a National Insurance number.
she holds herself in strips
of old newspaper and homemade paste
tries to follow the instructions she's been given   *get plenty of rest*
          eat milk, yoghurt and kale   change your knickers at least
once a day   try including weight-bearing activities where your feet and legs
support your weight like walking running or dancing   balance   an
apple   on your head   talk to other people going through the same thing
          talk to a doctor before taking herbal supplements   rename
the bees they don't like the ones that you gave them   give up holding delicate
objects in your hands   turmeric! have a cold drink   tried yoga,
tai chi or meditation? insert a hormone ring into your vagina   have another
 cold drink

                    no-one told her
                    it would be this sharp,
                    the great big secret held inside
          the Matryoshka dolls that came before her,
                    look at them
                    lined up on the sideboard
                    arranged large to small
                    each vessel a variation

of the original,
all with bulbous bellies
flushed cheeks, pursed lips,
she is the smallest
solid, chunky, the only one
that hasn't been split open.

1994

In the school choir she sings
Life is a Cabaret Old Chum
for the teacher who died
from a secret disease,
the hall smells of pencils
ashtray and Dettol,
all the dads are angry
they punch holes in the dry walls.
Crammed on the stage
she wears white tights
borrowed from a classroom enemy.

Every afternoon at 4pm
she watches two films,
one is about a dirty princess
who is friends with mice,
the other features a haunted teacup.
On Fridays she trots up to the 20p machine
selects a plastic ball filled with gunge
presses her thumb into the slop
to make fart sounds all weekend.

2016

One long synth note
signals it's the morning after a big party
wide-angle shot of the clouds (time lapse)
the flamingo tinted dawn,
close-ups on pretty sweaty faces
the effects of a pill tapering off.
On the walk home she counts
11 new flags on her road
some are Jacks, others are Georges,
a chorus of tuts, the dawn roar of the A road
a Ring doorbell reports her
for door-knocking.
In her constant quest to be an outsider
she forgets that she too
is part of the white masses,
she thinks she should talk
to more old people
(as long as they are not her parents)
to try and understand
where they are coming from,
she balances a coffee cup
on her brand-new laptop
just to feel dangerous.

2034

She has sold another collection
of clay Matryoshka dolls
lips scratched open
in elaborate *sgraffito*,
when you un-lid each one
glittery intestines spill
from their bellies.
She moves all her old beginnings
into a brand-new flat,
out-of-date tins of chocolate milk,
an orange balaclava, fettling knives,
a jam jar full of dead bees.
The last morning on the boat
she unfastens her jaw to draw in the soggy earth
watches a dog carry a duckling in his mouth,
he thinks he is saving her from drowning.

2042

Catastrophe has once again
pierced the soft middle,
the weekend kids are marching.

you did us dirty! you murdered the water! too dry to grow bread!

Warmed by their love
of exclamation marks
she designs the front cover
of their pamphlet.

photo mosaic of young faces make up the word NO!

She carves a diorama of the protests
out of Babybel wax –
a minor celebrity straddles the Murdoch statue,
young girl with a pineapple updo
squares up to an officer with enlarged hands,
toddler banging a pot
all the glistening figurines with chain link arms
by morning they're a burgundy pool.

1991

The war brings her cousin for a visit.
They sleep squished in her bed
like *dolmas* packed in Tupperware.
Cousin notices the size of the cucumbers
so much bigger over here
one can feed a whole family.
The mums buy them matching shoes
the magic ones with the key in the sole.
It's their first proper snow
but they're unsure how to play in it
didn't know it would be so wet.
The excitement kills Stacey the gerbil,
they crunch through icy ground
a Barbie-sized hole
use a shuttlecock in place of a tombstone.

2035

Look at her, a homeowner
in the last heat-proof block in Clacton,
she sells herself on the idea
that her hard work got her here,
Dad was born in an asbestos shack
mum is a snail.
With the abundant light she sets up still life photography scenes:
      socks drying on the radiator
            frosty tumbler of banana wine
                perfect ramen egg
She takes up the trapeze
cultivating large biceps
beneath gently sagging skin
her collagen is depleting
and she doesn't give a fuck.
Meanwhile, a man from Moscow
shoots the last white rhino
a pigeon makes a nest
from old cable ties on the balcony
she monitors mum's oxygen remotely.

2050

She is commissioned to make a set of plates
commemorating the return of the wolf.
Curved and rimless they depict
a pack of she-wolves and a flock of sheep
in a beauty parlour. The alpha has her nails done
an iridescent pewter, an ewe blow-dries
her curly wool straight.
She tests the set on her friends,
spoons scraping against porcelain
an unctuous helping of rabbit stew, real butter
they gulp moonshine from matching flutes.

1985

Her first birthday and mum is awake
5:22am, the time she was born.
Mum plants a kiss on her fuzzy head
to mark year one. Mum will execute
a variation of this kiss in the coming years
will peek at the door frame
as baby grows from snoring piglet
to a lumpy teen in fold-out futon.
Later, scheduled emails the subject line
happy birthday baby! nothing but two Xs in the body.
The aurora tone of WhatsApp notifications
a pixelated bulldog blowing out candles
timestamp – 5:22am
and finally, hand-delivered packages
filled with limes and mezcal,
instead of cake a challah covered in hummus
one fat candle.

2043

When her weekend son is angry
she encourages him to throw bagels
out the window when he smashes
the soup bowl they glue it together
Kintsugi-style a golden repair when he tears
off the wallpaper by the bottom bunk she sticks
cardboard frames around the exposed patches when
he quietly aches for some unknown thing she doesn't know
how to give she rubs his back into the blue
morning when the nightlight fails
when there is no more cheese she posts bouquets
of white tulips to her friends, children now grown.

2053

Her stomach no longer respects breakfast
but her body clock has shifted to dawn hours
for the first time in her life she witnesses consecutive sunrises.
She hosts a lunch with a company of long-lost cousins
fries lettuce in lab-grown fat, sets placemats in order of age.
One complains about the flood migrants
they're technically closer to France than London!
Incredulous, as if the apricot clafoutis was attacking him.
Another cousin claims the government is bankrupt
after all the space flights,
they are trying to trick us into speaking Russian!
Gripping her jaw like a jockey riding a spooked horse
she stares at the egg box monsters on the mantle.

1989

The guppy gobbles up its babies
frenzied tiger-print tail
Teacher blocks the tank with her body
then, a science experiment –
they wrap one sandwich in foil
and another in cling film
to see which is waterproof.

In circle time she says
jelly is her favourite food
even though she's never had it,
too much bone.
Everyone else has an imaginary friend
when they ask about hers
she lies. Says her imaginary friend
is called wiggly wormworm
um, he works at Kwik Save
has seventeen children
and he is tired all the livelong day.

2060

When she stretches her calves on a park bench
when she chooses a yoghurt from the cart
when she ambles down the supermarket aisle
she is transparent as rice paper, assumed to be wispy,
her self-image doesn't match the reflection
in the bars of the trolley. She asks a boy of 20
where they keep the bean powder
and he dials himself to top volume
OVER THERE BY THE MEALWORMS.
He doesn't know a collage of her cunt hangs in a gallery.

2038

She prepares boxes for Mum
who will only eat fruits of the home counties,
charred aubergines, baked peppers,
guavas that stink of armpits.
She witnesses slices of the foster kids' milestones –
reading an old-fashioned clock,
sprouting hair in damp places.
She slips crustless sandwiches and deodorant
into their backpacks, puts crispy
sheets on an extra hot wash.

Her mind has always been
a thousand open tabs
a patchwork quilt with every square urgent red
a pot of brown lentils on the boil
thick bubbles spurting
but now a cool liquid
floods her veins like kefir.
Assisting the transitions of the tender lives
in her orbit locks her serenely in place,
all the calm and grace of a grey heron
stood on the bank of her river.

2017

Self-care has entered the lexicon.
It's cute to ignore texts
to post a pic of a bubble bath and a rosé.
Therapy is the new rock n roll
but more expensive
she remembers the free councillor from uni
wonders if he's retired to his house in Looe.
She thinks about bread, her old nemesis.
Her employers think she's five years younger
pay her accordingly
we 👏 do 👏 this 👏 job 👏 for 👏 the 👏 love 👏 anyway!
On the commute she feels a searing kinship
with an elderly woman
who eats three cereal bars back-to-back,
face obscured by a church hat
everything crisp (except the shoes).

2047

After another cremation ceremony she tries
to get her shit together on a hazelnut farm,
it's raining tomatoes and every time she tries
to catch one in her upturned apron
it splats into red mist. She remembers
the retreat with the mushroom shamans
dressed as the Sugababes,
draws sharp breath whilst foraging for a magic formula
that can un-funk her,
joins the Amazon waiting list for the anti-ageing bacteria
found only in the soil of Easter Island.
It's so popular the earth is almost entirely gone
The Mo'ai have fallen into the ocean,
the unmistakable giant heads with slender noses
and curled pouts carved from solidified ash
momentarily float on their backs
as if they were relaxing on a package holiday lilo
before vanishing under a wave.

2039

She inherits

781 books (over half are in a language she can't read)

two boxes of unused face masks

a bottle of Chanel Number 5 (empty) that granny bought mum in '64

Teflon pots falling apart since the '90s infused with special aubergine essence

a Bulgarian ring worth less than it looks

7 kilos of rice

a rosewood chest that smells of ink and rage

large bowl of dried out pomegranates

and enough cash to get the fuck out of Clacton

un-daughtered un-moored no one stood between her and the sideboard edge

solid chunk in the Matryoshka line

un-split

2010

Now that planes have stopped flying
the chemtrail people
have nothing to believe in
start to blame the water,
they're right this time
it's been killing us all along.
A deli has opened in a former toilet
she is introduced to the word
Bresaola, discovers that some of her pals
wear crusty trainers by choice.
What does it mean to be an artist anyway?
An entanglement
with an undeformed part of herself?
She thinks she needs to suffer
to make Good Work
but her version of pain
is beans on toast and a half pint
instead of a full Sunday roast.
A chorus of tiny violins on her iPod
a long, thin, shiny receipt roll
advertising care work
from the dodgy machine at the jobcentre.

2052

The womxn in her building host a fayre to raise funds
for the flood migrant crisis in the West Coast.
One neighbour sells taxidermy fashion
a whole pigeon affixed onto a hat, resplendent wings
outstretched, like Victorian ladies who flaunted
birds of paradise on their heads – plucked from New Guinea,
dead parrots for sale, violet, butter yellow and cerulean feathers
spread across London, a market of open beaks.
Another neighbour sells cupcakes
in the shape of the crumbling coastline.
On her stall she flogs A6 postcards
decorated with pressed lavender and the shiny skins
of crisp packets, the words *message to past self*
handwritten in cursive script.

in the evenings she cooks prawns to feel like a grown up
even makes a soup from the heads quietly serving herself
the juiciest bits her socks are on the radiator for so long
they're crispy and stinky from dinner

living separately together with Boyfriend she holds a
respectable job with disrespectful pay making monsters out
of egg boxes with kiddies every morning at 5:48 the
neighbours alarm blares through the wall Boyfriend sleeps
through she bashes the headboard with the heel of her palm

when everyone else is having fun she is crouched on the
living room floor working on her oeuvre a tableaux of
female characters who are taking revenge on their savage
directors Shelley Duvall from *The Shining* bashes Stanley
Kubrick with a baseball bat Tippi Hedren claws out Alfred
Hitchcock's eyes *The Little Mermaid* strangles her dad
with her tail

2048

Having misplaced her Someone-hood
she funnels her energy into handmade films
they mean something again,
have earned a vintage charm.
She makes a Claymation short:
a worm with 17 children crawls
around a supermarket
sniffing out bargains,
he tries to shoplift a tin of soil
but remembers he has no pockets
to hide his loot in.

She teaches evening weirdos
how to spurt themselves on a sketchbook,
for an icebreaker she asks
which vegetable are you and _why?_
On Sundays she chugs dandelion coffee
under the peach tree in the communal garden
vying for space with the pigeons.

2015

She has lost a lot
of weight from the new medication,
can eat only tuna
white rice and oranges.
She makes a note
of all the pals
who compliment her new loss.
Men find reasons
to touch her more often
like she's famous.
The camera they slip
into her anus
is smaller than anticipated
Nurse says the sedative is like
a couple of jolly gins
with the gals.
She thinks, no
it's like a small lick
of something powerful
from the corner of a baggy.
When it's over
she scoffs a family-size trifle
on the tube.

Her new art project:
a line drawing of a vulva scrawled
in the steam of bus windows
she films six second videos
of them flickering in the rain
uploads them to a micro blogging site
that has only one year to live.

She listens to radio lectures for fun -
A quarter of all under-25s will grow to be 100.
All eating must be clean.
All foetuses start off as female (a penis is born from a clitoris).

She has known about the internal
clit for a while. What other reason could there be
for those primal eruptions beneath the surface?
Every time a friend locates theirs
she feels a smug wave of ecstasy
there is so much to talk about
so many plans to make.

2054

Some of the weekend kids
now taller, prepare a savoury birthday cake
in the shape of the number 70.
They have assembled a slideshow
for her headset, a selection of frames
from their thriving and messy lives.
Entering the 3D reels
she counts two babies,
one giggles at a redheaded figure
holding two bagels up to her eyes,
the other squishes a crustless sandwich.
She repeats the clip of her weekend son
holding a decorative roll of paper
mouth in the shape of a lightning bolt.

2025

Is it time to launch an OnlyFans?
She could specialise in lime green sex,
throwing gunge on herself
whilst singing themes from '90s adverts
for men who cultivated their sexuality
in front of Nickelodeon
could wear an orange balaclava
to conceal her identity.

2045

The weekend kids remain the same age
she regresses into a bootcut jean
a t-shirt with a radical slogan
wishes for a shaved line in her eyebrow
but she owns property now
it wouldn't look right,
stares at the SAD lamp so long
it fucks her eyes
she can finally get glasses,
chunky frames pointed tips
she wants to be mistaken
for a graphic designer
with Swedish ancestry,
clean lines in her flat
heavy table ornaments.

2003

She swipes an old Nikon from dad, who in turn nicked it from work. Takes hundreds of close ups: her friends' vaccination scars, a shiny baby clown fish, the green sign outside Lucky 7 – *céad míle fáilte, gaelic football, hurling.*

At the protest she waves her camera like she's a Someone, somehow ends up behind the barriers, police mistaking her for press. But she's out of film, two left on her reel – she snaps a 10-year-old covered in 'No' stickers, a slab of cardboard with *drop pills not bombs* written in felt tip.

She visits ancestral Europe, a stowaway on a Balkan rave bus. Stops at a mountain monastery, Battenburg facade. The technicolour frescoes explode off the ceilings: a bat-winged demon licks a woman's ear, a dog with human limbs weighs a man's soul, a bearded grandad is spliced in two from crotch to head.

Then, a week at a techno freeparty, a beleaguered line of portaloos, few soft furnishings, the dogma of the original old skool geezers an unexpected lesson in ageing. A brief romance with ketamine turns her limbs to soup.

2041

She lifts an art deco lamp
from a decaying lover
who says her anaemia
is sexy, wonders –
should i take close ups of my bruises?
should i draw more vulvas?
After becoming
s o m e o n e
the next casing is
v e r y i m p o r t a n t.
Scared she is running dry
she flogs another bottle of vitamin D
from her stockpile to buy herself time
tight walks in the neighbourhood
pacing amongst brutalist ghosts
shaking a horse-chestnut tree
in case an idea should happen to drip down
from its candling flowers.
The city parks are muzzled
the kiddies that were given speeches and megaphones
at *tRUth sEEker* congregations
are all grown up.

2011

Her and Boyfriend trip through America
high off each other, palms full of credit cards
they share an ice cream in the shape of The Buttes
at Monument Valley, pass a billboard
that shouts *Guns Gays and God*
a handwritten poster outside a record shop
London Riots! 15% off band shirts.

In the foothills of Sangre de Cristo they visit
an adobe church with twin bell towers
come to Jesus clouds, a sandwich board instructing them to
Turn off your cell phone and connect with Him.
The holy dirt, burnt orange and running out
fills the pilgrims store bought containers
by the exit, abandoned crutches and a feedback book.

2061

She soundproofs the flat with Tena Lady
reserves bathwater for the window box.
Making a plain omelette she remembers
the egg and spoon race at school,
they were given plastic eggs to save them
from breaking. For the sack race they cut
the bottoms off for safety
a swarm of kids holding hessian rings
round their chests running squeaky on laminate.
At Easter they ate chocolate because
it's the same colour as the big wooden cross.
She tops up the bowl of sugared beetles
she keeps by the door
should a weekend kid decide to visit.

1992

Teacher talks
in a low voice
when she welcomes
the new children to class
something wrong
in their home countries.
They stand at the blackboard
the girl in tight plaits
plastic bobbles
the boy is allowed
to keep his hat on.
When they chat
in their own language
at playtime she listens in,
indulges in the close-together Ks
the heavy Ls almost the same
as how granny talks.

At lunchtime they play
mad cow disease
it's like normal 'it'
but when they get caught
they shout moo,
spin in a tight circle
like the dry leaves that whizz up
in miniature tornadoes
from which they gather debris
to make nests for the birds.

2044

She had always been so smug
about her godlessness
wore it like fox fur,
but the chubby little heartbeats
that fill the weekends
make her think differently
she dips a toe into a Friday night candle,
special bread, builds a shrine
to the bees she once knew.
Why would her ancestors bother to count
the seeds of pomegranates
unless they thought she would be
the repository of all their efforts?
Persecuted for so long
did they ever conceive she would be
the last one on the sideboard?
The only adversity she faces –
an increase in service charge
to cover the cost of the communal corridors,
paying extra for plus-size trousers,
a lover who so badly wants
to smash up her sculptures
but bottles it at the last minute.

2057

A retrospective of her work –
a series of cardboard frames
around holes punched directly in the gallery wall,
Easter Island faces carved into soap,
the dog with his Dorito, blown up to the size of a billboard.
She clenches everything by the Babybel buffet
the loves of her life, half here, half missing,
assembled like the remaining Spice Girls
take turns to squeeze her hand,
drip feed her warm sav blanc
what the fuck is she going to do next?

2063

She was pregnant once,
a boy ate a sausage roll
in an old carpet factory
then what?
A computer voice
reciting stories
in a made-up language?
All languages are made up.
She voicecalls a friend
who is flat on a rug
fresh great grandbaby
fingering his nose
mucky and lovely
bubbles in his mouth instead of words.
Staring at the window she notices
a passing drone filtering the golden hour
through its propellers,
a fleeting camera obscura
splashes onto her wall
and for the first time in her life
she tries oil painting.

2040

She always wanted
to be a street chronicler
recording outsiders
snapping clay freeze frames of beautiful
and desperate creatures
wanted her day to day to be a lived documentary,
imagined painting herself
into a bohemian corner
with all the romantic trappings:
early arthritis from the damp in her loft,
a lover that burns her
most important work. But she realised
the only thing she could log
was how horny she was on a particular day,
what she wanted to eat.

She moves into a womxn-only complex
on the right side of the floodplain
an ex-church with exposed brickwork
tall radiators, a communal reading room
with a steep triangle roof
all signs of sermon vanished.
In her bedroom
a rose window that won't open
spills morning light in shades of Jesus red
onto her rustic bedspread.

1996

To make her mark at big school
she has pierced her nails,
takes another step away from her body.
A boy from the blue table
throws fake vomit at the teacher
latex circle with maroon chunks
like a pizza that's been left in the sun.
At her first sleepover
she forces her friends to watch her
mime the harmonica solo
from the Spice Girls song.
She has a real harmonica (dad's)
but won't make the sound,
with cold metal against her teeth
she holds her breath and dances.

2055

She takes on extra classes
lecturing on the importance of sifting for ideas
in the neighbour's bin.
Her pension is delayed again
but bucket hats have made another comeback!
Scouring the wardrobe for saleables
she finds a box of flared leggings
remembers a time of no pockets,
she's down to the last candle
voicecalls her neighbour for a match.

1997

The hearse is expected
to pass through the high street at 11ish,
mum takes granny, who doesn't understand English but
it's history we have to at least see it.
The neighbour went to sign the book
godresthersoul. But she is old enough
to be left alone in the house.
Masturbating like a maniac
she keeps the windows shut despite the cloying heat,
when she silently climaxes her nostrils flare
and catch the synthetic grape
of a burst bath bead in the bedside drawer.

2049

She is making more films,
splices together stock footage
accumulated from her youth:
In a sea life centre a girl does a backflip
a dolphin behind glass copies her.
In a classroom a girl with plaits and a blurred face
assembles an assault rifle.
In a home studio a girl unboxes a baby doll
dressed in a sharp business suit.
She has never before addressed
her loneliness, the songs of her heyday
informed that her duty was to be untouchable,
she films a self-portrait sequence:
her naked gingerbread body
swirls to the harmonica solo
from *Say You'll Be There* by the Spice Girls,
on her head, a papier-mâché mask –
the magnificent horns of a wild goat.

1998

She soaks through the toilet paper
wedged in her pants
p a n i c   a hasty jumper round her waist
her clenched gait through the corridors.
Late for lesson in the computer room
Sir shouts. Careful not to plonk
damp buttocks on the seat
she perches at the edge
of a wheelie chair.
Tampon instructions
say lie back knees up
it's easier to insert,
she's never seen a bathroom floor
big enough to lie on
foetal on the tiles
she ruins her blow-dried Rachel.

2008

Three months into the internship
she thinks, *I could really do this,*
organise the team-builders
couple citybreaks a year
order a large glass of white wine
in the gallery bar on weekends.
She is gifted a bottle of perfume
from a corporate sponsor
skin lacquered with syrupy fruits
eats more bacon in one year
than she has in her entire life
takes mum to see films with subtitles.
One is set in a warzone but
is not about war –
five women meet every week in a salon
balmy gossip under the bonnet dryers
legs sticky with caramel
one lady is fucking the other's husband
the youngest pretends she's a virgin.

2018

She sends Boyfriend a poo emoji whenever he is on the toilet. They have their established sides separated by the beefy pillow she uses to prop up her knees. She has named all the lamps, Leonardo, Colin, Duane Benzie. He Blu-tacks a birdwatch pamphlet to the window. They play rock-paper-scissors with their eyes, grow leek tops in nothing but water, over mist the B&Q bonsai pretending it is a hungry baby. She reads a blog about a wife who watched an entire episode of *The Chase*, memorised all the answers and re-watched it with the husband. The tap is broken again, but he finds a way out with an elastic band. He wears a cap indoors, just for fun, learns how to make a ramen egg, she practises different styles of lying down.

2062

She has deleted her need to be v e r y i m p o r t a n t
landed on notable footnote.
An occasional lover wants more.
It doesn't matter how much she has accumulated
in the cupboard of her achievements
doesn't matter that flares have died
and come back again and died again
there is always a man expecting a washed plate,
a warmed vest. She makes herself an angry sandwich
leaving a pile of filthy bowls in the sink.

1995

She's suddenly aware of her middle,
how it swells and oozes
clammy in a tie dye t-shirt.
She fails the other girl's tricks,
the way they pull the bottom
of their t-shirts through their necklines
to make a make-shift bra.
Sweat gathers in her belly button
bodyrolls by the swings in the lemonade dusk.
The adult's favourite hobby is to talk about her body
Don't keep the biscuits on the top shelf she'll only grow taller.
For homework Teacher makes them learn
about Archimedes by weighing themselves with bathwater
remove the liquid litre by litre and write up the total.
Teacher makes them read their measurements
out loud. Hers is the largest number,
Teacher jots it all down on her clipboard and sighs.

2020

There is a flour conspiracy.
A collective clenching
of bum cheeks.
Her pals share recipes
and some personal news…
some start to believe
the circular messages,
say things like
makes a lot of sense when you think about it
shut their windows tight
to keep safe
from government helicopters
spraying the air with disinfectant.
There are men she knows
who have waited
their whole boyhood
for an apocalypse,
studied gun tutorials on youtube,
slayed zombies in training
but now the end is finally here
all they can do
is refuse medicine,
build barbecues.
She wants to murder
the phrase   *going for a walk*
the end of the world
is something that happens
over there, her first actual catastrophe
threatens the soft middle of her
gingerbread figure,
she panic buys a hula hoop
makes herself a martyr
by writing endless to-do lists

                                    gather all the paracetamol

        from the cupboards
                                        to make a fire

curate the sheets
                                    of toilet paper

            make an inventory
                                                of breath

unclench your jaw
                                without medicine don't panic

        break into the old tins
                                        (special-offer corn)

with teeth
                                    made weak

            from all the clenching
                                            save all

        the rusty pounds from the abandoned   shopping trolleys

    melt them down
                                        into a name necklace

        (choose a name
                                    more popular than

your own)   ignore the woman in cash converters

        the coins were worth more before   *you did this to them luv*

2046

Friends face sickness whilst she runs
scabless and unprotected
gambling with her lungs at underground
dinner parties where she is the oldest,
fried turnip paste and bean curd in communal dishes
potcheen in mismatched mugs,
all she wants is warm sav blanc,
to crawl topless across the floor.
Sticky sideways sleep she dreams
her belly has become a large ball
of maggots and they are humming
so loudly it's like the girls
are calling her home.

2058

Sick of repeating her old story
she records all the things she has learnt this year:
a recipe to make a candle from old crayons
a new route to orgasm
which student's artwork to tickle her friends with
the times to avoid her pigeon neighbour
how to ration her pre-work coffee
an affirmation to let her weekend son go
the temperature gauge on her fridge,
after 18 years she finally knows
the lower the number, the colder the milk.

2006

She wears granny's nightgown
for the procedure,
a friend from the raves
is the porter.
Head down he wheels her
to the biscuits
unable to sit
in the exit room
her boyfriend arrives late,
sausage roll pastry
flaked on his hoodie.
She moves house again
un-guarantored has to pay
six months' rent
upfront in cash
in the move she finds a
crumpled drawing
of a gingerbread figure
with the word *ME*
in the middle,
in her room
there is finally a bed
big enough to spread out
out all her mandatory reading.

2056

She can no longer keep the biscuits
on the top shelf
but even with the bone loss
she is taller than the average woman.
She chalks around her starfish body
like a corpse in a cop drama
drawing concentric outlines
within and outside her silhouette,
a blast radius of the self,
iridescent jelly baby,
electric gingerbread figure,
all the little girls she contains sellotaped together
to make one big shrunken woman.

2065

For dinner she airfries
a hamless sandwich
in bed with an eye mask
she tunes into Russian news
understands few words but takes comfort
in the heavy Ls and close together Ks,
thick as cow cream.

1987

She grips daddy's jowl
dangles frankfurter legs
over his shoulders
a giant at the end of the world
though the air smells too fertile for Armageddon
fresh and damp with mulch.
They jump over fallen trees
walk the full five miles to nursery
the bus route blocked
by an upturned Volvo.

Acknowledgements

Huge thank you to Aaron Kent, Charlie Baylis, Stuart McPherson, Emma Kennedy, Cathleen Allyn Conway and to the entire crew at Broken Sleep. I feel very lucky to be part of the collective and I'm so grateful for the values you bring to the industry.

Big love to Alice Frecknall, Bridget Minamore, Elisabeth Sennitt Clough, Jemima Foxtrot, Maria Ferguson and Shruti Chauhan for providing encouragement in the earliest stages of this idea, thank you for helping me to grow into a better writer.

Special shout out to Bryony Littlefair, Cecilia Knapp and Toby Campion for the care and attention you gave to these poems, you helped me carry them past the finish line. Thank you so much for your time and insight, you are my hologram Sugababes.

Thank you to Steven Camden aka Polarbear, Roundhouse and Rubix for kickstarting the journey all those years ago. Thank you to Arts Council England for supporting my time to complete the manuscript.

Thank you to my wonderful friends, I know I turn into a hermit when I'm 'working' (staring into space, willing the words to come), I love you all so much.

To mum and dad, thank you for still letting me raid your fridge and your bookshelves. To my Jamie, I think you are the very best.

LAY OUT YOUR UNREST